THE DIARY OF AN ADOLESCENT

SAKSHAM CHUGH

XpressPublishing
An imprint of Notion Press

XpressPublishing
An imprint of Notion Press

No.8, 3rd Cross Street,CIT Colony,
Mylapore, Chennai, Tamil Nadu-600004

ISBN 978-1-63633-364-9

This book is in the Reverence and the Loving memory of My Grandmother whom I lost recently. It is only with her blessings that today I am able to write this book. I dedicate this book to all the people who helped me ,motivated me and supported me. I would like to thank My Parents, My Brother and My Grandfather for always motivating me. My immense gratitude and appreciation to My School, My Respected Principal Ma'am and My Teachers for continously being the guiding force. Last but not the least Forever Thanks to The Almighty for making this possible.

Contents

ONE
CHAPTER-1

September Saturday

DEAR DIARY-

I am not used to this stuff but still I want to write it. So, diary let me tell you how we met. I and my Mom went to supermarket. We both just took the stuff we wanted and then I went to the book section in search of comics. Soon after my mom came to the book section in search of me. There was a lady I don't remember her name but she was a colleague of my mom but she looked very old. The appearence of her son was quite weird and indeed he was a naughty boy. When we were in the market that boy just opened a pack of chocolate and ate it without even telling anyone. I think I didn't care until that women who rather than scolding her son started talking about me to my Mom. She said that your son looks quite different and naughty and I was just about to tell her the incident but I controlled myself. Then my mom and that lady talked for hours as usual about their children's habits. That lady was just talking about her child that how great he is. You may seem that I am exaggerating but she was talking about her son like he is going to be the future Prime Minister of our country because she assumed that her son had amazing qualities. One of the quality that she was praising about again and again was that he writes a journal everyday and that has transformed his personality. out of all the qualities of that child, writting a diary is what inspired her and bought a journal for me too. I refused and asked her not to take that but she didnt care about my refusal. To be honest My mom doesn't even listen to my father so how could she listen to me. You know how Moms are. Then she just ignored me at the store and behaved like I am an anonymous person. Then while we were driving home an incident happened. The Tyre of our car got punctured and my mom doesnt really know how to change tyre and there was no help nearby. We called our dad and he said he will come in some time. So rather than wasting time standing under the sun we both decided to go for a lunch. We went to a nearby Sub Store. My mom bought me a burger from Sub Store. I was happy as I was eating a burger after long. But my happiness was quite short lived. My Mom told me that the *burger I was having was not a treat from my mom but I had to pay from my pocket money. Since I thought it was my mom treating me I had bought the most expensive meal. My entire pocket money was wasted on that meal. I was sad. My Dad came and finally the tyre was changed. As we sat in the car I realised this punctured tyre had cost me my entire pocket money...Oh My God...What the hell Mom you shouldnt have done this to me... Oh I Wish our car didn't breakdown. When we reached home I was lost in the thought of not being able to spend a single money in school as I have lost my pocket money and was tired so just tried to sleep. Suddenly my mom called me and asked me to start writing a daily Journal and If I did so she would increase my pocket money.*

You know what, like all of you out there I can do anything for pocket money. So I started writing my diary and here I am writing my first Journal. My day was just like any other day, teasing my little brother, playing with friends, visiting the Supermarket and Eating at Sub Store. I will introduce my friends to you tomorrow. Oh I forgot!! Tomorrow is a holiday so I am going to sleep the whole day. Honestly No...rather that burger not only gave a hole in my pocket but I realised i am gaining weight so I have to wake up early tomorrow to exercise. So Bye for now good night and sleep tight!

Bye!!!

TWO
CHAPTER-2

CHAPTER-2

September,Sunday

DEAR DIARY-

Hello diary, as I told you yesterday, I will introduce you to my friends so let me fulfill my promise. I have mainly three friends and we all play together. My Best Friend is Sam. You know diary why sam is my best friend because we both are Crazy. I first met him in our classroom but I think I just ignored him. But then I met him when my family planned a trip to a Water Park. So finally after convincing my parents that I will study hard and even if you want you can take my pocket money they took me to a water park. It was indeed a very average place to hangout. The crowd was in large number and I wasn't really enjoying much. Suddenly I heard someone calling my name and when I turned around It was a crazy looking guy Sam. I don't know how he got my name. I gave him a weird reaction and somehow we could connect with each other. Finally after spending allot of time together we became good friends. I realized not only we but even our parents could jell around well. I think I enjoyed the company of Sam and we both started spending time together. Not only at school but we both enjoyed spending crazy time even after school. We became best friends. He was a typical best friend. He would always put me in trouble. Whenever I did not do my homework and he did it, he would make it a point to tell Maam to collect our homework for checking and put me in trouble. Not just once but I realised because of him atleast once a week I would be in trouble.

Now let me tell you about my second friend Fred. He is a great friend unlike Sam who puts me in trouble. I think I can consider him as my "Bestie" if he leaves the habit of being a book worm. Yeah he is a book worm and yet my friend too. He is very smart But I don't know he is a little bit different than Sam or maybe a lot different. Hope he will understand me some day. But yeah he is a kind person. Thankfully he doesn't put me in trouble. He does save me *a lot of time as he has the habit of doing the same task again and again so I am able to take his help for homework. You know Diary why even after helping me so much he is not my Best Friend because he is a Bookworm and sometimes bores us a lot.*

Now lets move on to my third friend his name is Sasuke. I consider him as my best friend too. Yeah its weird I have three friends and two of them are my Best friends. But leave it let me tell you about Sasuke. He isnt gentle at all he always try to misbehave in the class and makes the class look funny that's why he is my best friend. You know he makes fun of everyone in the class. Everything that happens in the class Sasuke will find a reason to make us laugh. He is the Kapil Sharma of our Class. He will make everyone laugh even in front of Ma'am. Sometimes when Ma'am is in a real bad mood somehow he will create a light atmosphere and Ma'am would cool down. You know what I have a secret to share we went on a school picnic recently and he carried a mobile phone with him. We secretly clicked alot of funny pictures. I am sure when we grow up and look back at these pics we will have something to reminisce about. I am happy to have these crazy and freaking friends who are always ready to help each other. But yeah I don't have any girlfriend yet so phew leave it I don't want to have a girlfriend. I have so much to talk to you but its late I think I should end today's journal. Today was a normal day and just nothing much happened. But still my days with my friends are always my special days

So bye for now.

THREE
CHAPTER-3

September, Monday

DEAR DIARY

You know I have been thinking off late to give you a name. A name I can connect with. I have been sharing so much with you, my experiences, funny friends and talking to a Diary sometimes makes me feel awkward so I thought I should give you a name. Ok let me think a name for you maybe Serah yeah Serah would be a good name for you so from now on I will call you Serah. Wow!! thats a nice name I wished my parents were updated as well and kept a nice name for me too. Ok serah so I will tell you about my day. Today was my school so I woke up at 6 AM. Then I ate my breakfast. I ate cornflakes with milk. Then I changed my clothes and wore uniform.

My grandfather dropped me to bus stand and as usual I was late and when I boarded the bus I was the last one to enter and couldn't find a seat for myself. All the seats were occupied. Even our Conductor uncle was standing. There is something good about Sasuke he does make fun of people but he does respect elders a lot. So he gave his seat to Conductor uncle. He is an old man. Then the bus started. We both were standing. He again started creating fun zone around me and we kept on laughing. After some time we both had an argument as I had given my notebook to him and he forgot to bring it to school. Now our Science teacher will scold me. He behaved as if nothing has happened and told me try to manage for one day. I really felt bad. When we reached school and I realised our first period was Science and Maam wanted to collect our Notebooks for checking. Alice maam our science teacher, asked us to submit our notebooks. Sam as usual was the first one to keep his notebook and again wanted to put me in trouble. But today something different happened . Something I never thought could happen. These crazy friends of mine saved me from our Science teacher. All of them got up and said Maam I have Sid's notebook. To our surprise Maam punished all four of us and even though we were punished and were standing outside the class we had the best time as we all were together. She scolded us but we four continued enjoying ourselves. Though I thought it will be the worst day today, but it became my best day again. And then as usual we four Musketeers did a lot of fun together not only in class but also during lunch breaks. We planned to have a pyjama party together soon. We all wanted to plan a night stay at each other's house. Then suddenly the bell rang and Fred told us that we all should rush back to our class or we will be punished. We all started running back to our class and we had a race, as usual Sam was the last one to reach and he got scolded by our teacher. He is the Crazy Couch Potato of the group. The day was all fun filled when we all are together. It was two and then we left for home. I did my homework and since we have to catch up in the evening again So I don't leave anything pending. When I was about to leave to play with my friends I saw my dad coming home. I waited to wish him but to my surprise he said come in I have something to share. As I entered I heard my dad inform my mom that he is taking us out for Dinner as my dad has got his dream project. I went to my dad and said I want to take my friend as well. He agreed but my Mom started cribbing. She said its an expensive place and we should not take our friends.

After convincing her for good one hour she agreed to take my friends. That was the biggest mistake of my life. I called them all and we met in half an hour outside my house. We all fit ourselves in the backseat of my grandfather's car. My mom dad and my brother went in a separate car and we went with our grandfather. It was fun and we reached the restaurant within half an hour. Now the trouble started. My Best Friends created a lot of problem for us. Sasuke and Sam had a fight for the seat and they broke few glasses. That was just the beginning. Everybody at the restaurant gave us a stare. It was very embarrassing for my parents but my grandfather supported us. Then Fred Dropped his plate with all vegetables. Though he did apologise but there was alot of scene. Now my parents started giving me a stare and I promised them that it wouldn't happen again. The dinner arrived and since we all were hungry we gobbled upon the food and left from the restaurant paying less for the food and more for the damages.

FOUR
CHAPTER-4

September, Tuesday

DEAR Serah

New day with new beginning.. Woke up at 6 AM had my exam today. Since I was not prepared well I realised I have high fever. I went to my Mom and she immediately checked my temperature and told me its just the Exam Fever and not high temperature. I saw my brother making fun of me. I did tease my brother and did tell him that I am high with fever but no one was listening to me and I had to go to school. Dad dropped us to school today as we had missed our bus and told us that we should write our exam well. My brother who is a Prodigy told Sure dad and I was as usual embarrassed. Then with heavy heart I entered the school. I met my three other musketeers and told them that I was down with fever. I thought they would empathise with me rather they made fun of me. We reached the classroom Fred told Maam that I was unwell. So Maam told me to give the exam in the Medical room alone. My only ray of hope - My friend whom I thought would help me as I was unwell was also removed. I entered the medical room with heavy heart and darkness in my mind. The nurse at the medical room gave me a comfortable seat to write the paper. My teacher came and gave me the paper and I realised I knew almost everything. Now I was feeling better and I wanted to go back to my class but now my Medical teacher did not allow me to go back. I was shattered again. But I gave my paper well. My friends keep coming to the medical room with some or the other excuse. They did ask me if I need their help but I told them I will be able to manage. When I reached back after submitting my paper, I saw everybody discussing the question paper. I realised half of my paper was incorrect. I and Sam both were now down with fever as only our answers tallied and everybody else in the class had a separate answer. We both again started feeling the fever. Now Fred came and made us feel comfortable. He said that its okay we will get marks for steps. I wish atleast 50% of our steps should be right. We both reached home and did not talk to anyone my mother gave me lunch and asked me about the paper. I told her I have given the best paper in the class and will get just a few marks less than Fred. It was fun as Mom thought that my paper had gone well and she let me and my brother play on X-BOX. I hope my mom doesn't have to face my real paper and someone could correct few answers for me. I just wanted Mom to feel good my intentions were not bad. Bye for now Diary I think I am getting that fever again....lol...

FIVE
CHAPTER-5

September, Wednesday

Dear Serah

Its been few days that my exams have ended and I knew we would get to see my answer sheets in the school today. As usual I didn't want to go to school due to the fear of facing the maths teacher with the answer sheets. So again I had a nice excuse I went to my Grand dad and told him that I want to go Shopping with him. I told him that there is some function in the school so if I didn't go to school it wouldn't make much of a difference. My dadu did think for sometime but later disagreed and I had to go to school. When I reached school everyone was excited for the Maths paper except me and Sam. We both knew that we are going to get the least marks in the class. So we both sat together hoping if someone could save us today. Fred and Sasuke were having a gala time as their answers were matching with the rest of the class. I and Sam were silently praying if someone could save us during this difficult time. We waited for the Maths period and wished if Ma'am was on leave. Sam took me to staff room to check and there she was our Maths teacher Miss Preeti. She saw us and called both of us in. She asked us to pick up the exam bundle and take it to the class. With lot of courage we picked up the answer sheet and went to the class with Ma'am. She asked us to keep the papers on the table. We kept the papers on the table and went to our seat. She announced in the class Sid and Sam please come out. We both thought that may be we have failed and Maam wants to discuss about our marks in front of the entire class. Now again with lot of courage we both reached close to maam. Miss Preeti told us that few questions we had attempted quite different from the entire class. The entire class started laughing and we felt very embarrassed. Miss Preeti scolded the entire class and said that did I say that they have attempted it wrong I just said that they have attempted it differently. She asked us to write down the formula and explain it to the entire class. We both wrote the formula and explained it to the entire class. My Maths teacher actually realised that we both have created a different formula for solving these difficult problems without wasting much of the time. She was very happy with us. We both were on top of this world. Nobody in the class could believe that we have become Mathematics Ingenious. I realised on that day sometimes when we hate something it is only our inner fear that is stopping us from working hard. Once we start loving our problems they become more of our way to reach beyond our imagination. Who would have ever thought in my class that someday I and Sam the most mediocre students of the class would develop a formula for everyone else to solve various mathematics problems without wasting much time. My Maths teacher called at my and Sam's home and congratulated us for our achievement. My parents were expecting a call for my complaint but this call changed their way of looking at us. I thanked almighty for making me feel that yes if we want to do something in life we need the will and surely some luck. Since in our school we do have regular prayers and assemblies it is imbibed in us to have good moral values so all my friend and our teachers did offer our prayers and then we partied in the canteen. It was indeed the most fun loving day. A day in the morning I thought will be my worst day but it actually turned into my best day. My Maths teacher is trying to get my formula registered. She did say that even if it doesn't get registered you both are my achievers. Bye for Now serah I hope we keep getting big achievements for our *school*

SIX

CHAPTER-6

September, Thursday

DEAR Serah

After all the achievement in the school and lot of appreciation at home I was all set to go to School again. My fears are now my strength. I was excited to meet my friends as I and Sam have gained a lot of appreciation from everyone in the school. Not only our Maths Teacher but also our Respected Principal Maam who was going to acknowledge our efforts today in the school assembly. So I took out my new school Uniform dressed up neat and tidy and was all set to reach school. Today after such a long ti me my younger sibling..the so called Prodigy was envious of my achievement. Not only he but also my Friend Fred and Sasuke who never expected that I and Sam could do something ever were appreciating our work. Thanks to the formula that we created. It changed our life. I was on cloud nine. I reached the Bus stop on time and today everyone there wanted to talk to me. Now as I boarded the bus I had lots of my seniors coming to me and Sam and talking to us about our formula which could even help them as it was an interesting shortcut that could help everyone solve the mensuration problems with lots of ease. We reached school and Sasuke as usual created a fun atmosphere in the class. We were enjoying ourselves. Our class teacher came and informed about the special assembly that we had to attend. We were all excited and as we reached the Auditorium we wished all the teachers and the assembly started. It all started with regular prayer and then Our efforts were acknowledged by our Respected Principal Ma'am. I was almost in tears.. The tears of Joy which came rolling from my eyes because today was the day I never thought would ever come in my life. Sam was equally elated. My friend Fred and Sasuke too were emotional with us as even they never thought that someone from our group could do something like this. As we have always been the four Musketeers. Serah there are some moments in life that not only bring you happiness but they change your lives forever. This was that moment. Now I wanted to *justify our achievement and I promised myself that I will transform my life for better and create a name for myself. The assembly ended in a very happy note and we sang National Anthem with immense Patriotic Feeling.*

During the lunch break we musketeers decided to do pyjama party at Sasuke's house today. After convincing our parents we reached at Sasuke's house at around 6PM and started with all the fun activities. We played games ordered food from outside and infact Sasuke's parent were too cool and they helped us organise our Pyjama party. It was good fun. While we four were partying at around 11 PM at night we could feel something unusual happening outside the house. There was some noise coming from the lawn and since his parents had already slept early we could feel that there was an intruder. I was frightened to the core acted that we should just lock our door and ignore what is happening outside. Sasuke too felt the same and said that we should act as if we are sleeping. Fred the bookworm of the group and Sam said we should rather go and check who is outside. So we flipped a coin and there it was heads as asked by Sam. So now we had to go and check. We all gathered a lot of courage and opened the door and found that there were two ladies looking for the leftover food that we had thrown in the garbage outside our house. They appeared to be extremely hungry and were eating some leftover food that we had thrown. I really felt bad and wanted to help them. We went near the window and told the two ladies standing outside that we want to give you food. The ladies told us that we have two children with us who are also equally hungry. Seeing them all we felt too bad as we just throw food without even caring about anything and suddenly we had someone who was ready to eat from the bins. Sasuke and I cooked six packets of Maggi, poured them in disposable plates and served them all from our window. They grabbed the food as if they had not eaten from days. The children were as old as us and were very thankful to us for the food we gave. We even gave them our cake that we had kept in the refrigerator to eat tomorrow. We felt so good giving them food. When we asked those children if they studied in some school. The children replied that they have never been to any school. We felt too bad for them. I remembered my promise in assembly today to do something better in life. I asked my friends if we could do something for them. Now we told them from tomorrow we will teach you and give you some food everyday so you can come and study with us. These children and their moms were very happy. They all blessed us and left from there. It was indeed an emotional moment and all of us realised how lucky we are. We sometimes crib and complain to our parents despite all the luxuries we get in our lives. Today we four Musketeers promised that we will not only study for ourselves but also give meaning to the life of those children. Seeing them eat from the bin made us value food. We all promised never ever in our lives will we waste food rather we also plan to make a Charity Food fridge. This fridge will be for anyone hungry and not being able to buy food. People from all around can come and keep leftover food packed in this fridge. Anyone in need can take the food. We also promised that we would take atleast one hour everyday for teaching those children who are not able to go to school. With this promise and lot of hopes we ended our party. All four of us understood that the real meaning of life is not to be selfish but to do something for those who have not been as lucky in lives as we are.

Bye Serah today indeed was a very meaningful day as it changed our lives forever. I hope we keep up to this thought an do something for them.

Bye See you soon with more fun experiences..